Success with Less Stress

Success with LESS STRESS

Rachel Moore

First Published in Australia in 2017 by Rachel Moore
Copyright © 2017 by Rachel Moore
The moral right of the author has been asserted.

All rights reserved.

No part of this publication may be reproduced, stored in a retrieval system, or transmitted in any form or by any means, without the prior permission in writing of the publisher, nor be otherwise circulated in any form of binding or cover other than that in which it is published and without a similar condition including this condition being imposed on the subsequent purchaser.

National Library of Australia Cataloguing-in-Publication entry

Creator: Moore, Rachel Ann, author.
Title: Success with less stress / Rachel Moore.
ISBN: 9780648138709 (paperback)
Subjects: Stress (Psychology)
 Self-help techniques.
 Success.
 Well-being.

Printed and bound in Australia, United States or United Kingdom by IngramSpark, Lightning Source Inc

Table of Contents

Introduction — My Story 1

Strategy 1 — Sleep 11

Strategy 2 — Take a Break 19

Strategy 3 — Emotional Intelligence 32

Strategy 4 — Mindfulness 40

Strategy 5 — Minimalism 47

Strategy 6 — Find the Time 54

Strategy 7 — Not Procrastinating 62

Strategy 8 — The Voice in Your Head 69

Strategy 9 — Engage a Coach or Mentor 78

The Difference This All Makes 86

About the Author 90

For Noddy and Bailey.

Noddy, thank you. You have always been my greatest supporter.

Bailey, my beautiful daughter. You are the love of my life.

Introduction — My Story

In my work as a consultant, I come across a lot of people who are working hard (nothing wrong with that!), but who unfortunately are extremely stressed and on the verge of burning out. They are often working long days, juggling a range of responsibilities and feeling guilty for a bunch of things (insert your own guilt here…). My guilt was not spending enough time with my daughter.

I often recognise my past self in many of these people and feel quite a lot of empathy for them and the stress they are experiencing.

In my case, I started actively making changes to reduce my stress levels and to focus on my own version of success.

It worked ☺

I am living my 'current' version of success (success looks different to everyone and can be very different at each stage of our lives) and have dramatically reduced my stress levels.

The idea of this book is to share some of the strategies that I practise and teach. I have experienced firsthand the benefits of these strategies and seen many people achieve the success they seek after putting them into practise.

A bit of background

I have been working since I was 14 years old, when my parents told me to go out one Saturday and not come home until I had myself a part-time job. I started working at a local bakery every Saturday morning. About a year after that, my parents told me that they had found me a Sunday morning job at a pharmacy in a suburb that was two bus trips away. I can't even remember what time I had to get up and leave the house every Sunday morning to catch the two buses to be at the pharmacy in time for opening. I spent the rest of my high school days working each weekend and throughout the school holidays. Maybe this is why I then spent the bulk of my adult years working a minimum of two, sometimes three, jobs and more often than not, undertaking study at the same time.

Fast forward about 30 years and not much had changed. I found myself working long hours due to a combination of working two jobs, renovating (yet another) house, studying (always studying!), and 'balancing' motherhood with a partner who worked long hours. As a shift worker he worked nights, weekends and public holidays, so on average we were able to spend a day together as a family one Sunday a month. Deep down I kept telling myself that I wanted more time with my daughter, but at the same time I was focused on ensuring a certain standard of living. I wanted to be sure we could afford her school fees, comfortably meet our mortgage(s) and take regular holidays. And yet, who had time for holidays! Working two jobs meant that I had no annual leave available as I was always using any leave I accrued in my full-time job to work in my consultancy business.

Whenever I mentioned to friends or colleagues that I was thinking of slowing down and finding a better work/life balance they would smile one of those cynical 'sure' smiles and laugh — like you ever will!

A few years ago, I was diagnosed with a general anxiety disorder. That shouldn't have come as any surprise really considering the rate I was working at and the guilt and worry I always felt. Every challenge comes with an opportunity though, and the opportunity here was to learn practical ways to reduce my anxiety and then use those techniques to reduce my stress levels.

As I started reducing my stress levels and anxiety, I started giving considerable thought to what 'success' meant to me. It took quite some time to work it out as I had never really taken the time to think about it before. Seriously, I thought about this for at least two years.

Naturally, success means different things to everyone. As a young adult, success might mean achieving certain study results or getting our first car. As we get a little older, success may be about living in a certain location, getting a promotion, achieving a particular job title (like CEO or Doctor), or hitting a specific figure in regard to salary. On the other hand, success can be climbing a mountain, travelling to a destination you have dreamed of for years, having a family, making the team, winning an art prize, publishing a book, finishing a marathon, or learning to walk again after a serious accident.

At this stage of my life, I realised that success to me meant: doing work that I love, my business being financially sustainable, spending quality time with my daughter, and travelling (for leisure) regularly. Once I realised what was important to me, I was surprised to find that it was so much easier to make important decisions. By way of example, I had spent quite some time (again about two years) trying to decide whether I should focus on my work as a consultant (where I am able to focus on work that I love, but where the financial rewards can be ad hoc) or stick to the financial security of being an employee.

Then, my daughter was diagnosed with Autism. After the initial shock of receiving her diagnosis, suddenly the choice between consultant and employee for me was very clear. Of all the elements on my 'success' list, spending quality time with my daughter suddenly shot right to the top. The type of work I planned for my consulting business would allow me to do exactly that. I would spend more time working from home and it would allow me to work around her school hours and term holidays.

So, at the moment, I can say that I am 'successful'. I am doing the work that I love, my business is currently financially sustainable, I am definitely spending more quality time with my daughter, and we are enjoying more holidays and short breaks. At some stage in the future, I fully expect my definition of success to change, and when it does, I know that the strategies I have put into practise will mean I will be able to achieve that new success goal with a lot less stress. These are the strategies I talk about in this book.

The benefits that come from these strategies are two-fold. Practising them will help you achieve the success you want. At the same time, they will certainly lower your stress levels.

As you read through the success and stress management tips in this book, please be sure to start with the end in mind. Remember, when you first start exercising you are not going to be able to run a marathon. To keep your focus on what you should do and why you should do it, keep a clear picture in mind of what your health, personal life or career will look like when you achieve what you are setting out to do.

So, before you even start to read through the various strategies in this book, take some time now to note down what success means to you. This might come easily if have a clear picture of what it means for you and your circumstances. Or you may not have actively thought about this in the past, so it may take a little longer to define. That's ok. Remember, I spent a couple of years thinking about it!

> Success for me is/will be…

Many of the success and stress management strategies in this book will appear to be common sense and you may find yourself saying, 'I already know that'. If you find that is the case, I would ask you to keep an open mind and honestly reflect on how well or how often you are actually implementing these strategies. Some of them may be simple, but it doesn't mean that we put them into practise. Knowing is not enough. Just think about the last time you wanted to do something like improve your diet, cut back on caffeine, or start an exercise routine. Changing our habits takes time and effort. Start small. I don't recommend that you try to implement all of these strategies at once. It is also not necessary to implement the strategies in any particular order;

however, I would honestly recommend starting with the strategies in the chapters on *Sleep* and *Taking a Break* first if they are areas you could improve. Other than that, I encourage you to select strategies where you feel you will receive the most immediate benefit and start by investing your energy and focus into them.

The most important thing is, if you are feeling you are not achieving what you would like to achieve and/or are dealing with too much stress in your life, then try something different.

Let's Talk About Stress

> *'It is not the strongest of the species that survives, nor the most intelligent that survives. It is the one that is the most adaptable to change.' Charles Darwin*

I love this quote. It reminds me that life is all about change. Things change day to day and even moment to moment. Some of those things we have control over and choice about and some we don't. This book is a practical resource that can enable you to move through life's changes and unexpected events with a lot less stress.

Before we get into the strategies for Success with Less Stress, let's take a moment to talk about *stress*, what it is and how it is impacting us.

Stress. It is a term that we all use, sometimes on almost a daily basis, but what actually is it?

When we talk about stress in a medical or biological context, it is a physical, mental, or emotional factor that causes bodily or mental tension. The thing about stress is that it is a natural part of life and absolutely everyone on the planet has felt stress at some point. There is good stress that can invigorate us and move us towards our goals, and there is bad stress which if left unchecked can be extremely detrimental to our health, relationships and careers. There are so many events, circumstances and situations in life that can cause us stress. I could easily fill a page or two in this book on the various causes, but the focus here is not what causes stress, but on how to reduce unhealthy stress while working towards achieving your version of success.

The impact on our minds and body of extended stress is serious and wide-ranging. We can often see the physical symptoms that result from stress, but it can be harder to recognise the mental symptoms. You may have heard of the flight-or-fight response, which is also known as the Amygdala Hijack. The amygdala is an almond-shaped section within your brain that is responsible for your experience of emotions. You actually have two amygdalae. Apparently if you were to stick a pen in your ear and another pen in your eye, where the two points would meet, you will find your amygdala (please don't try this!) So, getting back to the fight-or-flight response: this response is a primitive survival reflex. Basically, if something such as a person, event or environment is threatening you, your brain decides within a millisecond whether your best chance of survival is to run away (flight) or to defend yourself (fight). You heart rate speeds up, your body floods with adrenaline and your breathing increases to give you more oxygen, all of which primes you to run or defend yourself.

In our prehistoric caveman days, this stress response would mean the difference between life and death. If a sabre-toothed tiger (why is it always a sabre-toothed tiger!) was running at you, you had to decide very quickly whether to fight it or run from it.

These days it isn't sabre-toothed tigers that are causing us stress, but events such as the way someone spoke to us in a meeting or a seemingly never-ending 'To Do' list at work. Our brain, trying to make sure we don't get killed, sees potential danger almost everywhere: in a grumpy partner, a micro-managing boss, a new job, a traffic jam, a long line at the supermarket, an unappealing reflection in the mirror — you name it. In reality, these events are not necessarily life-threatening, but your brain is still working to protect you by reacting as if they are.

I am going to ask you to think about how you currently view stress and to potentially start perceiving stress and your stress responses in a slightly different light. Have you ever watched an old movie where someone falls into quicksand and the more they struggle, the quicker it sucks them under? If you should ever find yourself in this situation, struggling is actually the worst thing you should do. If you have learned to swim, you may remember being taught that if you feel like you are getting into trouble, the best thing to do is lie on your back, spread your arms and remain as calm as possible, allowing yourself to float on the surface. Of course, it's easy for someone else to say, 'stay calm and don't panic!', but for you in that instant, maybe not so much. At that moment, your brain is screaming at you to try and escape from this dreadful situation. The problem is, that if you do keep struggling, eventually you will become exhausted and sink below the surface.

The key to this? Recognising when your brain has gone into threat mode and give yourself the space and capability to more consciously choose your response. Implementing the strategies in this book will allow you to do this.

At the end of each chapter, I will suggest various actions you can take or resources you can access in order to further develop that particular strategy for Success with Less Stress.

Strategy 1 — Sleep

> *'The amount of sleep required by the average person is five minutes more.'* Wilson Mizener

How true is this quote! How many times have we woken up only to have the first thought that goes through our head be 'just five minutes more' before hitting the snooze alarm?

The first strategy I am going to suggest you review in order to achieve success with less stress, is to get more good quality sleep. Wait, what? Yes, that's right. In order to be more successful and to achieve your goals, I am going to ask you to spend more of your precious time sleeping.

On average, we will sleep for 36 percent of our lives. If you live until you are about 90 years of age, you will sleep for approximately 32 years. Yes, you read that right, 32 years! This, according to Russell Foster, a circadian neuroscientist, tells us that sleep is a critical function and not something to be taken lightly. While sleep consumes about a third of our lives, most of us know little about why we sleep. In fact neuroscientists are still researching and debating the reason for this much-needed activity.

The exact reasons for and benefits of sleep are still not really known, however, there are some long-standing theories of sleep which include:

- *Inactivity theory.* That sleep keeps us out of harm's way at night time. (When you think about that, it is not that likely. If danger was coming, I would rather be awake to know about it.)
- *Energy conservation theory.* That sleep reduces our energy demand and expenditure. (In actual fact, we only conserve the energy equal to the energy in a hamburger bun, about 460 kilojoules or 110 calories, so this is also unlikely.)
- *Restorative theory.* That sleep provides an opportunity for the body to repair and rejuvenate and for the brain to clean itself of the toxins that built up during the day. This theory has waxed and waned in popularity for many years. There is some evidence to support this.
- *Brain plasticity theory.* That sleep is needed for memory consolidation, brain development and enhanced learning ability. This seems to be the most popular current theory with neuroscientists.

What *is* known is that sleep disturbance can create some dire consequences for:

- *Emotional regulation.* A lack of sleep impacts our moods and emotions. This tends to result in overt negative behaviours such as irritability, anger, substance abuse and poor dietary choices, all of which can have flow-on (and usually

undesirable) results. We will talk more about the impact our emotions have on us in the chapter on *Emotional Intelligence*.
- *Cognitive ability*. When we are sleep-deprived, we have a significant drop in focus and our ability to maintain appropriate attention on the task or goal at hand. We become more impulsive, and this impulsiveness is rarely positive — we are more likely to blurt out what we are 'really' thinking or engage in more risky behaviour.
- *Health and wellbeing*. A lack of sleep has been shown to reduce our body's immunity to illness, starting with an increased likelihood of catching a cold to increased risks of cancer, cardiovascular disease, diabetes and metabolic issues.

Ok, so I am sure that most of us would prefer to avoid those negative consequences, but how does sleeping help us to achieve our goals? Arianna Huffington in her TED Talk 'How to succeed? Get more sleep' suggested to the women in her audience that the best way to succeed was to 'sleep their way to the top'. An obvious pun and play on words, however sleeping (literally sleeping, not the innuendo in her comment) your way to success is a very real and practical strategy. Let me explain.

How Sleep will help you achieve Success with Less Stress

You will have more energy

Can you remember the last time you woke up from a good night's sleep and you felt refreshed, alert and ready to take on the world? For many of us, it might be hard to remember such a morning. When you do wake up truly refreshed (and not having to drag yourself out of bed), you have the energy to achieve more of what it is you want to achieve that day. Whatever it is that you want or need to do that day, will come so much easier. You are less likely to procrastinate or to be distracted from your objectives. Plus, you will feel great!

You will be more productive

For some people, spending more time sleeping feels counterintuitive. They believe that to be more productive, they should be using every spare minute working on their goals. Not true. Being sleep-deprived will reduce your productivity regardless of your determination. Having a good night's sleep will increase your brain's processing ability and therefore your productivity significantly, allowing you to achieve more in less time with your improved focus and clarity of thinking. A good night's sleep will not only allow you to 'get more done' but you will achieve more in less time, giving you more time for the other important areas of your life, such as family or 'me time'.

You will be happier

Ok, that sounds nice, but will being happier help me to achieve my goals? Absolutely it will! Happiness is one of the most productive states we can be in, as explained by Harvard Psychologist Shawn Anchor in his book, *The Happiness Advantage*, and his TED Talk, 'The Happy Secret to Better Work'. He explains that when our brains experience what he calls 'The Happiness Advantage' which is your brain feeling positive, you perform significantly better than when you are feeling negative, neutral or stressed. His findings include that your intelligence rises, your creativity improves and crucially, your brain is 31 percent more productive when feeling positive. 31 percent! Who wouldn't want to increase their brain's productivity by 31 percent on any given day?

You will make better decisions

You have most likely heard someone say (or you may have said it yourself) when trying to make a decision, 'let me sleep on it'. It turns out that there is more to this than it being a turn of phrase or delaying tactic. There is actually some science behind good sleep and making decisions or solving problems. Scientists have found that when you sleep, your brain looks for a solution to your problem or for your decision. You may have experienced this yourself, when at some stage you have woken in the morning with the answer to your previous days' problem or question clear as a bell in your head. Even if you don't wake up with an answer to your problem, that good night's sleep will increase the capacity of your brain to evaluate your decision or problem with improved clarity.

You increase your odds of a PB or climbing that mountain

If your success goal is related to physical or athletic performance, such as running a marathon, achieving a 'personal best' time or climbing a mountain, sleep will improve your performance. Several studies have shown that when athletes (of many differing persuasions) get more sleep, they improve in areas such as speed, reflexes (reaction time) and accuracy.

You're less likely to get ill

I don't have time to be sick! How often have we heard that or said that ourselves? No-one enjoys being ill. The reality of life is that no matter how well we look after our diet or wash our hands to avoid germs, we are going to get sick. One way to reduce the frequency of illness is to get more sleep. Carnegie Mellon University found people who sleep less than seven hours a night are nearly three times more likely to catch a cold. This is because a lack of sleep can suppress your immune system, which makes you more vulnerable to infections.

Strategies for Sleep

DO

- *Manage your environment.* Is your bedroom or sleeping space conducive to getting a good night's sleep? Your room should be cool and dark, and where possible, free from other distractions such as noise (like the 'ping' of a Facebook alert from your phone).

- *Switch off the technology.* At least one hour before you wish to fall asleep. Yes, it is tempting to do a final check of your emails or watch just one more episode of your current Netflix binge-fest, but turning off the blue lights of your devices will help your brain recognise that it is time to start winding down and be ready for sleep.

- *Create a sleep schedule.* Where possible, go to bed (without electronic devices!) and wake up at the same time, even on weekends or your days off. This will help your body clock to regulate and fall asleep each evening.

READ

- *Thrive* by Arianna Huffington. Published 2014. Harmony Books. US

WATCH

- TED Ed — *What would happen if you didn't sleep?* by Claudia Aguirre

You can find all the talks listed in this book on my website – successwithlessstress.com.au/resources/.

As I mentioned in my introduction, knowledge isn't enough. Simply knowing what to do doesn't mean we will actually do it. If that was the case then no-one would smoke, eat junk food or binge drink. With that in mind, take a moment now to write down at least one strategy that you can and will implement related to sleep that will allow you to move closer to achieving your success goal or goals. You can select a strategy from the list under Do, you can decide to read or watch one or all of the recommended resources or you can identify your own strategy that will work for you.

It is also important to know *why* you are implementing this strategy, so there is a section for you to think about and write down how this strategy will help you.

Select a strategy from either Do, Read or Watch, or create one of your own and record it on the next page.

A strategy I will implement…

How will this enable me to achieve Success with Less Stress…

Strategy 2 – Take a Break

> *'Almost everything will work again if you unplug it for a few minutes… Including you.'*
> Anne Lamott

The next thing I suggest you do is take a break. Seriously?!?!?! First, I asked you to get more sleep, and now I am suggesting you need to take more breaks? You might be asking yourself, 'Just when do I get the time to achieve the success I want if I am sleeping more and taking more breaks?'

Ah, that's the kicker – most people think that in order to achieve their goals, to be more successful or even just to manage their heavy workload, that they need to 'push through', work harder, spend more time 'at the office' etc… Actually, the really bad news is, that working through lunch, taking work home, studying all weekend, or whatever it is that you continue to focus on for extended periods of time, is actually moving your further away from your success goals rather than closer to them.

You might be thinking... but I am too busy! I don't have time to take a break! Ah, if I had a dollar for every time someone said to me that 'they don't have time'... Sorry folks, but you actually do. 'I am too busy' or 'I don't have time' are nice, convenient and sociably acceptable excuses that we tell ourselves and others. Whether it be taking a break (lunch or a holiday), starting or finishing something, or taking up or re-engaging with a favourite pastime or hobby, 'I don't have time' isn't really the issue.

Let me give you an example. I met a woman recently who told me that she wants to start a movement and would do 'if only she had the time'. I won't go into details in case she ever does decide to start it but it was a really simple movement and a good idea as well. I have no doubt that the movement would be agreeable to many people and to get it started she would need to undertake no more than setting up a Facebook page or group and a having a few short conversations. The movement itself wouldn't take a time commitment of more than a minute each day if someone was actively participating in it. Interesting, isn't it? So, for this woman, is it really time that's the issue or something else? I believe that if you make the time you will find the time. I really can't imagine that this woman cannot find 20 minutes out of one single day in her life to set up a Facebook page or group and cannot find a couple of minutes on any given day to have a quick chat with people to explain the movement and her goals.

Let's bring this back to taking a break, whether it be during your working day or getting away from the rat race for a while. Many of us wouldn't hesitate to take a break after an hour or so of physical exercise, and most people with a regular exercise routine know the value of having a rest day as part of their schedule. But what about mental breaks? Most people don't consider the mental fatigue that they are experiencing in any given day or over a period of time and the impact that is having on their stress levels, performance and productivity. The fact is, the more hours you work, and particularly the more hours you work without a break, the less you will actually achieve. If you don't believe me, there was a study undertaken by John Pencavel of Stanford University in April 2014 on *The Productivity of Working Hours* that confirms this.

These days technology allows us to work from anywhere at any time. Which can be great (I love working from home). The idea is that this gives us flexibility and choices around where and when we work. Unfortunately, this also has a flip-side, which means many people are connected to their work (and not necessarily to their goals) every waking moment. This means they never really switch off and take a break. Naturally this continued mode of being 'on' is not good for stress levels and can actually reduce productivity and leave us too mentally fatigued to focus on our success goals. While many people feel that there is an expectation that they are and can be available anytime, regretfully for many of us, we have actually created this expectation all by ourselves. We just don't realise that we did this and think it has been caused by our boss, our industry or technology. This state of being constantly available ends up creating more 'work' and giving us less time to take a break and truly switch off.

I realised I had created that expectation myself while working for a financial services organisation. In this organisation, it was not unusual for employees to be sending and responding to emails in the evening or on the weekend. In fact, I can recall one night when I was sitting up with my little girl who was unwell. It was about 12:30am. She was lying in the bed with me and seemed quite settled at that point so I thought I would send a couple of quick emails relating to some actions that were on my mind (you know how it is… to get a jumpstart on the next busy days' workload). I guess I shouldn't have been surprised upon sending those emails that just a minute or two later, I received some replies (and no, not out-of-office replies — actual replies to my emails). The fact that people were replying to me at 12:30am, when they should have been asleep (we couldn't have all had sick children keeping us up that night!) really started to play on my mind.

A couple of weeks later, I decided to do something really quite radical and take the weekend off. No emailing, no reading of my emails and no replying. It was harder than I thought as I had created such a habit for myself. To ensure I wasn't tempted to do a 'quick check' of what had come through, I turned off the alerts on my phone. This has turned out to be one of the best actions I have ever taken. Not subconsciously listening out for the 'pings' of a new email has done wonders for my stress levels and truly allowed me to take genuine breaks and focus on the things that I really want to concentrate on.

When I arrived at the office on the Monday morning, I had a few people approach me saying 'Hey, I sent you an email over the weekend. I am surprised that you didn't respond.' To each of them I replied with a smile, 'Actually, I decided to take the weekend off and I found I really enjoyed it, so I am going to be doing that more in future.' What do you think their responses were? Unequivocally, every single one of them looked at me and responded genuinely with 'Good on you!'. Every. Single. One.

The world hadn't ended. Disasters weren't looming. No-one had died (think about it; unless you are working in a field that requires you to literally save lives, chances are no-one will die if you don't reply to an email over the weekend). And honestly, if it was something that was so critically important, shouldn't the person call you if they really need you to respond or do something?

The benefits of my 'radical experiment' turned out to be two-fold. Firstly, I started to truly relax and enjoy my weekends without thinking that I needed to check my phone for new emails. This gave me more time to focus on my success goals including spending more quality time with my daughter. Secondly, and by far the most interesting result of this, was that people stopped sending me emails on the weekend. It simply just didn't happen anymore. It was at that point I realised just how much I had created that expectation in other people around my availability.

So, taking weekends and evenings off is great, but what about taking breaks during the day? Maybe if I am not working at night anymore, I should push through during the day to be sure I get everything done, right? Ah, no.

Ignore the clickbait that tells you that we have an attention span that is less than a goldfish. From the research I have undertaken, the general consensus is that the average adult can focus their attention fully on the task at hand for at best, 20 to 40 minutes. After this amount of time, our concentration wanes and needs to be rebooted.

The breaks that you need at this time are not the ones like updating your Facebook status or checking News.com to see what is happening in the world. Those are called 'distractions' not breaks. And honestly, I am guilty of these distractions myself. As I have been writing my book on my home PC, I have taken steps such as turning off Facebook and email alerts to ensure that as my concentration starts to dwindle, I don't take the easy distraction option. The best thing you can do is take a break that involves either moving or refuelling (healthy food or drink). And preferably if you are going to be eating, moving to a space away from your desk to do so.

'Don't worry about breaks every 20 minutes ruining your focus on a task. Contrary to what I might have guessed, taking regular breaks from mental tasks actually improves your creativity and productivity. Skipping breaks, on the other hand, leads to stress and fatigue.' — Tom Rath, New York Times bestselling author

Now, what about holidays and using that annual leave you have accrued? According to a 2015 Roy Morgan Research study, 28 percent of full-time Australian workers had more than five weeks' annual leave accrued. Take a break people! I often have people say to me that they are too busy to take a holiday or even a short break. That genuinely makes me feel very sad. Thinking back to the expectations that we create, the only reason these people think they are too busy to take a holiday is because that is the story they are telling themselves. Look, how many of us work in such critical and specialised job functions or roles, where if we took a long weekend or, heaven forbid, a week's holiday, the organisation or business would completely collapse without us? Sorry, not sorry, but if you were to get hit by a bus, the organisation would somehow manage to struggle on without you. You are replaceable. Someone else can fill in for a day or a week. And if there is really no-one else who can do your job, then some serious consideration needs to be given to either a succession planning strategy, or, if you own your own business, how you can set up systems or processes that allow you to step away for a few days.

These days I schedule at least two actual holidays and at least one or two long weekend breaks a year. I run my own business and do not employee other people, so there is no-one to step in and do the work while I am away. My strategy? I plan the holidays in advance, book them in my calendar and then let all my clients know when I won't be available. Rather than being detrimental to my business, I have found this to be quite the opposite. My clients know that if they want to book me, they need to get in early around the times that I am working. Naturally I have built up good professional relationships with my clients, however I have found that by being clear and honest around my availability, they will provide me with all the flexibility they can.

In my early thirties (usually an individual's career-climbing years) I decided to take a year off from work altogether. I took a four-wheel drive, a boat and a tent and spent a year camping and fishing my way around Australia. What a wonderful experience that was! When the money ran out and it was time to come back to 'the real world' I had a twinge of concern that taking such a break early to mid-career would be detrimental to my job prospects. As it was, quite the opposite turned out to be true. Every role that I interviewed for when I returned to the workforce, I was offered a position. I ended up being able to choose which role and organisation I wanted to work in. My thoughts on why that was are around the fact that most of the interviewers were fascinated (and some admitted to being a little envious) about my year travelling. After such a great break, I was a relaxed and confident interviewee who had a whole bunch of new life experiences under my belt and felt completely comfortable in my own skin. This naturally came out in my interactions with the various hiring managers.

How Taking Breaks will help you achieve Success with Less Stress

You will have the headspace to re-evaluate and refocus your goals

According to Harvard Business Review: *'When you work on a task continuously, it is easy to lose focus and get lost in the weeds. In contrast, following a brief intermission, picking up where you left off forces you to take a few seconds to think globally about what you're ultimately trying to achieve. It's a practice that encourages us to stay mindful of our objectives.'*

Your creativity and problem-solving abilities will improve

Without a doubt, many of my best ideas have come to me while I have taken a break and been out walking. I have loved just 'going for a walk' since I was a young adult. I have always said, 'walking is just as good for my mind as it is for my body'. To back up my moments of 'inspiration' while walking, a Stanford University study found that walking increased creative inspiration by approximately 60 percent. '...*Walking requires a certain amount of attention but it leaves great parts of the time open to thinking. I do believe once you get the blood flowing through the brain it does start working more creatively.*" Geoff Nicholson, author of *The Lost Art of Walking*.

You will improve your memory and learning capacity

Similarly, as we discussed in our chapter on Sleep, taking a nap break during the day has been shown to improve learning, memory and increase mental alertness. Ah excuse me Rachel — that sounds very good and all, but, I can't take naps in the office! Hmmm, maybe not or maybe you can? Many offices these days have multipurpose rooms, alcoves or small meeting rooms that you can book and take a nap for 20 to 30 minutes during your lunch break. Trust me, I have done it myself and it did wonders. But don't just take my word for it. Some famous day time nappers include Bill Clinton, Margaret Thatcher, Sir Winston Churchill and Albert Einstein. In fact, research undertaken by NASA revealed that a 26-minute nap improved performance by 34 percent and alertness by 54 percent.

Your productivity will improve

Yes, just like getting more sleep, taking breaks will actually improve your productivity. A study undertaken by The Muse (a career resource hub), found that the most productive people work for 52 minutes at a time, then break for 17 minutes before starting work again. The reason is that if you work in 52-minute bouts you are able to stay focused and work with intense purpose. The 17-minute break is not to be used for checking LinkedIn or other tasks. You use that time to move and refresh. Besides, your bodies were never designed to sit for eight hours (or more!) straight.

You can reduce your risk of dementia

This relates to moving when you take a break, be it going for a walk or hitting the gym. Walking, for me, has always been a favourite pastime. Right from my younger days in my early teens through to now. I used to say that I thought walking was just as good for my mind as it is for my body. And guess what? Neuroscience now backs up what I thought all along. Research shows that those who move or exercise regularly, do decrease their risk of dementia. In fact, in healthy adults the risk is reduced by 40%! Now that's got to be worth going for a walk for?

You will be so much more interesting!

Conversation 1 — when running into an old friend 'Hi, Great to see you! How are you?' Friend 'Hi, so busy!' Me, 'Really? What have you been up to?' Friend, 'Oh you know… Work, work and more work…' Me, not being the slightest bit interested in their work, 'Ok, well it was lovely to see you. Bye for now.' End of conversation.

Conversation 2 — when running into an old friend 'Hi, Great to see you! How are you?' Friend 'Hi, so busy!' Me, 'Really? What have you been up to?' Friend 'Well we just got back from…' or 'I am writing a book on…' or even 'I decided to take up mountain climbing.' Me "Wow! That sounds interesting! Tell me more about it…' Much longer and much more enjoyable conversation for both parties.

Strategies for Taking a Break

DO

- *Find time to switch off.* Don't check your phone for emails or messages anytime you have a 'free' moment. If something is critically important, the person who needs you won't be sending an email or a text, they will call you.

- *Please, take a lunch break.* And take it away from your desk. Preferably away from your office completely. Even better, go for a walk; even better again, go for a walk in the park.

- *Book a holiday or even a weekend getaway.* Don't just plan it or think about it. Book it and schedule the break into your calendar. When you book a holiday, you will take the break. You can let your colleagues and clients know well in advance so any critical work can be planned around it.

- *Take an afternoon or midday nap* (refer back to Strategy 1 on Sleep). Download and use a Nap App. My favourite is Nap26 which was developed by NASA.

READ

- *The Third Space* by Dr Adam Fraser. Published by William Heinemann 2012. Sydney, Australia

WATCH

- TED Talk — *How to gain control of your free time* by Laura Vanderkam

- TED Talk — *How to make work-life balance work* by Nigel Marsh

Select a strategy from either Do, Read or Watch, or create one of your own and record it on the next page.

A strategy I will implement…

How will this enable me to achieve Success with Less Stress…

Strategy 3 — Emotional Intelligence

Let's imagine for a moment that you and I are work colleagues. We happen to be in the break room at the same time making our morning cuppa and I smile at you and say 'Good morning! How are you?' What would your response most likely be? Chances are, no matter how you are feeling, your response would be along the lines of 'good' or 'fine'. Why is it, that we almost always answer 'good', even when we are not? It is such an automated response and sadly it is pretty much the expected response. Think about the following questions:

- When asked how you are, do you consciously consider, in that moment, how and what you are actually feeling?
- In any given moment, can you intentionally recognise and then shift your feelings if needed?

If you confidently answered yes to both questions, then feel free to skip this chapter! Ok, but seriously, even if you did answer yes to both those questions, I am sure you will still gain some benefit from reading on.

The idea of *emotional intelligence* (EI) was popularised by Daniel Goldman in his book, *Emotional Intelligence: Why it can matter more than IQ* published in 1995. However, the competencies of emotional intelligence have been valued for many generations with Charles Darwin publishing a book in the 1870s on the role of emotional expression in survival and adaption (*The Expression of the Emotions in Man and Animals* 1872). So, while the term EI may be relatively new, the concept has been around for a long time. In fact, in about 350 BC Aristotle wrote: *'Anyone can become angry – that is easy. But to be angry with the right person, to the right degree, at the right time, for the right purpose and in the right way – that is not easy.'*

There are many definitions of emotional intelligence (EI), but in a nutshell, it is about how well you can recognise and manage your own emotions and the emotions of others. A study by Multi-Health Systems Inc. Canada of about 4,000 people (men and women) found that *emotional quotient* (EQ)* increases from your late teens, levels off in your early forties and then drops slightly past the age of fifty. With this in mind, a question that springs to mind is: can your emotional intelligence and therefore your emotional quotient be developed outside this norm? Absolutely it can.

Read any book, article or blog on EI and they will all refer to the need for good EI to ensure success in any part of your life. There is no doubt that enhancing your EI allows you to increase confidence, build more meaningful relationships and enhance your ability to respond to challenges both in your personal lives and careers. There are many examples of how EI development has positively impacted business success as these are the activities that tend to be studied and measured. In regard to individuals, I have seen this firsthand, through the people I have worked with to develop their EI and the dramatic difference it has made, allowing them to achieve their own versions of success.

As an Emotional Intelligence Practitioner, I could write a book on EI, however EI is not the sole focus of this book and I do believe there are a great many good books available currently on the subject. Instead, in this chapter, we will focus on the foundation skill of developing emotionally intelligent behaviour, which is *self-awareness*. Self-awareness is an essential competency for emotionally intelligent behaviour. Without creating a deeper understanding of our own levels of self-awareness, it is near impossible to achieve *Success with Less Stress*.

Over the years, I have worked with hundreds of individuals and many work teams to help them enhance their emotional intelligence and self-awareness. I can't tell you how many times I have sat across a table with a client who confidently advised me that they are very self-aware. In my experience, most people consider themselves self-aware. The reality can actually be quite different. According to Dr Travis Bradberry, co-author of *Emotional Intelligence 2.0*: *'Only 36 percent of the people we've tested are able to accurately identify their emotions as they happen. This means that two thirds of us are typically controlled by our emotions and are not yet skilled at spotting them and using them to our benefit.'*

So, what exactly is self-awareness? It is the ability to recognise, *in the moment:*

- What you are feeling
- Why you are feeling it

and most importantly answer the question

- Is what I am feeling right now going to help or hinder me?

How Self-Awareness will help you achieve Success with Less Stress

You will know what it is you really want

Work. Eat. Sleep. Repeat. So many people do not know what they actually want or what they really want to do. They allow their external environments to direct them, almost driving them into a comatose way of living. When we live like this, we are not paying attention to what is going on inside us, and therefore to what our real desires or goals might be. The more self-aware we become, the better we are able to identify what is going on inside us and whether or not any given situation or environment is really working for us.

You will be able to manage yourself and others well

I once worked with a General Manager in an organisation, who upon learning about her own lack of self-awareness, confided in me that she had never once given any thought to the impact her emotions were having on herself or her direct reports. Cultivating your self-awareness improves your relationships (both personal and professional). When you are self-aware you can recognise in the moment if what you are feeling is hindering you (or others) and then make a conscious decision to shift. We are able to manage ourselves and our responses more effectively and therefore reduce the potential of negative impacts on others.

You will be better placed to make decisions

Emotions can be conscious or unconscious and no matter how much logic seems to play a part in making some decisions, emotions always play a role. The more aware you are of your emotions at any given moment, the more effective you will be when making what appear to be fact-based decisions. Consider the following scenarios: You manage a small team. One of your team members comes to you with a request to bend the rules on a defined process for a customer.

In scenario one, you just came out of a rather heated meeting and are feeling frustrated by a lack of progress from the discussion. Not being terribly self-aware, you don't recognise the frustration you are feeling and tell your team member that 'the process is there for a reason' and that the rules must be followed.

In scenario two, when your team member approaches you, you have just come out of a performance review meeting with your own manager who gave you glowing feedback about your performance. You are feeling on top of the world and a little invincible right then. Looking at their request through your own internal rose-coloured glasses you say 'Why not? Rules are meant to be broken hey?' Now, the point here isn't about which was the right response in these scenarios. The message is to recognise the impact that your feelings are having on your decision-making capacity at any given moment in time.

Strategies for developing Emotional Intelligence

DO

- Ok, so the first one is a 'don't'. *Don't judge your emotions.* Recognise that emotions are a source of important information for us. We do not need to consider emotions as good or bad, right or wrong. When thinking about the emotions you are feeling, simply ask yourself, is this emotion helping or hindering me at this moment? If the emotion you are experiencing is not going to help you at that moment, then consciously decide to shift that emotion.

- *Practice self-reflection regularly.* Once a week, sit down with pen and paper and write all the emotions you recall feeling in the last 24 hours. The most important aspect of this exercise is to not judge the emotions you experienced. Simply ask yourself, did that emotion help or hinder me at that time?

- *Feel your emotions physically.* Particularly when you notice emotions that could be perceived as negative, such as anger, frustration or worry, stop at that moment and consider what is occurring in your body at that time. Are your fists or jaw clenched? Are your shoulders tight or your brow furrowed? By taking the time to do this, you will soon recognise your emotions 'in the moment' before you may have been conscious of these feelings.

READ

- *Emotional Intelligence 2.0* by Dr Travis Bradberry. Published by TalentSmart 2009. US

WATCH

- TED Talk — *Everyday Compassion at Google* by Chade-Meng Tan

Select a strategy from either Do, Read or Watch, or create one of your own and record it on the next page.

> * You may have heard the terms EI and EQ (emotional quotient) used interchangeably and wondered what, if any, is the difference? A simple delineation between the two would be that EQ (emotional quotient) refers to the measure of an individual's innate emotional intelligence, similar to an IQ level, while EI refers to their demonstrable behaviours.

A strategy I will implement…

How will this enable me to achieve Success with Less Stress…

Strategy 4 — Mindfulness

Would you love to have more time? Would you like to double your life? Sounds pretty good to me. ☺

Do you remember when you were a young child, say somewhere between the ages of six and eleven, when a year seemed to last forever? The school holidays, and in particular, the summer holidays seemed to last for a year? Now as an adult, the years seem to fly by. And every year seems to go by even faster than the last?

Well, I have a theory about this. Children are naturally mindful. They are not thinking about what happened yesterday, they are not worrying about what they are going to do tomorrow or next week. They are living completely in the present. Enjoying their day and whatever it is they are doing right in that moment. As adults, even when we are 'taking time out' we are still thinking about other things. The argument we had with our partner the day before, or thinking about what we have to do either later that day or when we return to work. The truth is, we are rarely ever truly 'present'.

Research by Harvard Business School has found that people are 'lost in thought' about 47% of their waking hours. According to their research, *'people spend 46.9 percent of their waking hours thinking about something other than what they're doing, and this mind-wandering typically makes them unhappy.'*

Our thinking is often consumed by the past and the future. From a mindfulness perspective, embracing the present is about learning to engage in the moment and be completely absorbed in what you're doing. Your brain can drive you crazy with its myriad of thoughts, and one of the tricks to reducing your levels of stress is to recognise that you don't have to respond to every single one. You can choose what you want to focus on.

Mindfulness is a Buddhist concept founded thousands of years ago. A modern explanation is as follows: *'Mindfulness means paying attention in a particular way; on purpose, in the present moment, and non-judgmentally.'* This is how it has been described by Jon Kabat-Zinn, the creator of the Stress Reduction Clinic and Centre for Mindfulness in Medicine, Health Care, and Society at the University of Massachusetts Medical School.

In more recent times, the western scientific community has become supportive of mindfulness and its relationship with our overall sense of wellbeing. Mindfulness is the ability to observe your thoughts and emotions without necessarily becoming them. This links back beautifully to emotional intelligence and the skill of self-awareness. Mindfulness (just like self-awareness) helps you to observe your emotions without judgement and assume an open, curious and problem-solving approach to managing them. By slowing down and living more thoughtfully and gently we have a greater sense of calm and wellbeing.

Mindfulness is not just about meditation and breathing or relaxation. It is also not about 'emptying your mind'. Some people mistakenly think that mindfulness or meditation is about not thinking about anything. That is not the case and Andy Puddicombe explains this well in his TED Talk, 10 Mindful Minutes, when he says, *'It's more about stepping back, sort of seeing the thought clearly, witnessing it coming and going, emotions coming and going without judgement, but with a relaxed, focused mind'*. Being mindful means being able to truly focus on the task at hand and be present. It means letting the thoughts that wander into your mind simply pass by, observing them as distractions and not becoming caught up with them. This helps you give your attention and full focus to the job at hand and be more productive. Incorporating mindfulness into everyday life and activity will allow you to develop a healthy perspective of the way you view the world generally. This enhances our sense of happiness, mental health and levels of resilience.

While I cannot lay claim to being an expert in mindfulness, I do practise five minutes of mindful and regulated breathing each morning before I start work. Practising regulated breathing helps improve your ability to manage stress. Slow breathing allows you to increase the variability of your heart rate to decrease stress, improve focus and build resilience. Your breathing rate affects your heart rate patterns, which affects how your brain deals with stress. And all these processes are highly interconnected.

While it's difficult to directly control your heart rate, or your brain function, you can control your breathing rate. By regularly slowing your breathing down, you can improve your heart rate variability, which will allow your brain to more effectively deal with the stressful situations you encounter. Even when I worked as an employee in an office, I would start my morning by spending time in an available meeting room, undertaking mindful breathing before going to my desk and starting my working day. After those five minutes, I always feel amazing. I feel alert, re-charged and ready to take on whatever it is I am doing that day. My head feels clear and my energy levels are great.

Often in my training programs or coaching sessions, when I suggest to people that they take five minutes out of their working day to practice a bit of mindful meditation they will tell me that they don't have the time. You don't have five minutes? Well actually, you do. If you have time to make a coffee, you have time for a little mindfulness meditation. Honestly, when you make time, you create time. Don't believe me? Try it and let me know how you get on.

How Mindfulness will help you achieve Success with Less Stress

Improved cognitive ability

A 2010 study that was published in Consciousness and Cognition Journal found that mindfulness meditation training reduced fatigue and anxiety. Significantly though, they also found that mindfulness meditation training considerably improved visuospatial processing (the ability to visually perceive objects), working memory and executive functioning (the skills that help you get things done, manage time and pay attention). The really great news? They found that just four days of training made this noteworthy improvement to an individual's cognition.

Reduced work-related stress

One of the most widespread benefits of practicing mindfulness is the tangible reduction of stress experienced by individuals. Countless studies have demonstrated that those who practice mindfulness experience reductions in stress, anxiety, depression, fatigue and a range of physical illnesses. Mindfulness has also been shown to dramatically decrease the risk of work-related 'burn out' and improve overall mental wellbeing.

Enhanced creativity and problem-solving abilities

Our minds are often full of incessant chatter. With a clearer mind, we are better placed to come up with solutions, to think laterally and become innovative. When we are not being mindful, it is easy to stay in learned habits of thought without question. Some of these learned habits can be quite useful, such as driving a car, or riding a bike. Other times, these learned habits can be detrimental to our creativity or ways of working, by blocking our resourcefulness and ingenuity. Being more mindful can re-engage our imagination and encourage inspiration for new and better ways of doing things.

Strategies for Mindfulness

DO

- *Start with an app.* Find five minutes (ok, find at least three minutes if five really seems too much) with an app that works for you. Some of my favourites are: MyCalmBeat, Smiling Minds and Headspace.

- *Walk mindfully.* Next time you are rushing to a meeting, slow down and practice purposeful walking. As you walk, simply be aware of the movements of your body. Notice your feet on the ground, each step that you take and the feeling of the air against your skin.

- *Breathe.* We breathe about 20,000 times a day, and yet most of us take little notice of this life-critical action. One of the simplest mindfulness techniques is simply noticing your breath, counting silently to seven as you breathe in, and counting silently to eleven as you breathe out. The beauty of this activity is you can do this anywhere and anytime.

READ

- *Mindfulness on the Go* by Padraig O'Morain. Published by Yellow Kite 2014. Great Britain

- *10% Happier: How I Tamed the Voice in My Head, Reduced Stress Without Losing My Edge and Found Self-Help That Actually Works – A True Story* – By Dan Harris

WATCH

- TED Talk – *All it takes is 10 mindful minutes* by Andy Puddicombe

Select a strategy from either Do, Read or Watch, or create one of your own and record it here.

A strategy I will implement…

How will this enable me to achieve Success with Less Stress…

Strategy 5 — Minimalism

'You can do anything, but you can't do everything.' Greg McKeown — Author of Essentialism

Recently I started exploring minimalism. My initial goal was to have an uncluttered home, however I am finding greater benefits through having an uncluttered life and a lot less distractions. Having fewer distractions naturally gives me more time to focus on the areas of my life that I truly want to focus on.

Minimalism is not about owning nothing. It is about being purposeful about your possessions. What do you really need and love? And then, basically removing the excess.

The reason I am talking with you about minimalism is not to say that you need to own less stuff (though, trust me, it does actually make things easier). It is to say that minimalism frees up our lives and our time so that we can achieve more. What I am suggesting is to adopt a minimalist mindset.

When I started to minimalise, I cleared on average at least two full garbage bags of unnecessary clutter each week from my home over a three-month period. And you know what? So far, I haven't missed any of it. Life is simpler and there is a lot less housework! Which naturally means, more time. More time for the things I want to do and love to do. The purposeful choices I started to make about what we have in our home, transferred into making much more purposeful choices about how and where I spend my money, time and energy.

Did you realise that you are potentially exposed to over 5,000 advertisements a day? Yes, 5,000! Between digital and social media, print (magazines/newspapers) and billboards or signs. That's 5,000 times a day you consciously or unconsciously get a message to buy something. Do you want some really scary stats? Maybe not, but here they are anyway. In 2012, Australians spent: $8 billon (yes that is billion) on beauty, $9.5 billion on gadgets and $5.1 billion on fashion. Wow! For those of us living in Australia, you might have seen the recent series, The War on Waste on the ABC television network. I don't know about you, but I found the series equally fascinating and horrifying in terms of how much unnecessary waste we all mindlessly create.

Affluenza is a term that you may have heard in recent times. It is used to describe the need to strive for ever-increasing material wealth. It describes that unfulfilling feeling we get when trying to 'keep up with the Joneses'. In a world that these days seems to quantify success by a persons' fame, wealth and status, it can be described as a socially transmitted condition with the symptoms being an almost uncontrollable quest to own and have more material objects. Just think about the queues outside the Apple stores every time a new iPhone is released. The reality is that the pleasure of a new purchase quickly fades following the rush of adrenaline from the acquisition. I mean, just how life-changing do you think the purchase of the latest iPhone really was for those early adopters? Much really? I doubt it. Whatever it was that you 'just had to have', the pleasure fades quickly, so how convenient is it that then each year there is a newer model of car or phone or tv that you can purchase and each season a new trend in fashion that you can fall in love with and just 'have to have'? This short-term pleasure fades even more quickly when you have the realisation that this purchase does not link with, or even has moved you further away from, your goals.

Every single day we are offered innumerable opportunities and choices as to how to spend our money, our energy and our time. They key here is recognising that we do have a choice and do not have to buy, participate in or contribute to everything. With a minimalist mindset, you can learn to say 'no' to the things that do not align with your vision of success. Now, I am not suggesting you become so absorbed with your own goals that you say 'no' to everything else. What I am suggesting is that you become more aware of the activities and actions that are cluttering up your mind and try a bit of a spring clean. You will feel so much better for it.

'Maybe the life you have always wanted is buried under everything you own!' — Joshua Becker Author, *The More of Less*.

How Minimalism will help you achieve Success with Less Stress

Clarity of mind

We often do not recognise the link between our physical possessions and our state of mind. Think about the last time you had a really good clean-up. Maybe it was just the desk in your office or a room in your home. How did you feel when you were finished? I imagine that apart from a feeling of satisfaction (or exhaustion depending on how much there was to clear up!), you felt a sense of calm and order. You most likely felt that your head was clearer and you were ready to refocus on whatever else you needed to think about or do.

Less stress

Whether it is your home or your desk that is now uncluttered, imagine either walking into your office at the start of the day or coming home at the end of the day, and not having to start with clearing all the clutter. It can be literally life-changing.

More purposefulness

When you clear the clutter from your head, and your home or office, something quite magical occurs. Your motivation returns or is enhanced. You are goals and direction become better defined as the fog of confusion about where to start first, begins to lift.

More time

And don't we all want more of that at various stages. To quote Joshua Becker *'Every single thing you own requires a little bit of your attention and time whether it be researching, shopping, cleaning, organizing, repairing, replacing, recycling, or working just to make the money to buy the new thing that you can take home to clean and organize and replace.'* Naturally, owning less and not having a mind full of cluttered thoughts, frees up your time for what matters most to you.

Strategies for Minimalism

DO

- *Start with a physical declutter.* Decluttering our physical possessions and our minds takes time so don't expect it to happen right away. Pick a room, or even just the top of your desk and remove the clutter. I don't mean re-organise it. I mean, actually throw away, sell or donate anything that doesn't add value to your life or goals. Sound's easy. It isn't. However, I can guarantee that it does get easier each time you do it.

- *Do a digital declutter.* Next time you find yourself mindlessly web surfing, jump into your emails and unsubscribe from all the unnecessary subscriptions, alerts and shopping promos. This will remove that sinking feeling you get when you open your inbox and see all those unread emails. You should only be receiving the emails that you need. Again, this will give you the headspace to focus on your goals.

READ

- Becoming Minimalist — www.becomingminimalist.com

WATCH

- TEDx — *The ten-item wardrobe* by Jennifer L. Scott

This TEDx talk literally changed my whole mindset about the quantity and quality of clothing I owned. Up until watching this, I owned literally hundreds of items of clothing. I had enough clothing to fill two rooms of our house and that was after making an effort to cut back!

Select a strategy from either Do, Read or Watch, or create one of your own and record it on the next page.

A strategy I will implement...

How will this enable me to achieve Success with Less Stress...

Strategy 6 — Find the Time

Do you need more time? Do you want more time to do the things you really want to be doing? Well, some tough love here: stop telling yourself and others that you are so busy. The reality is, if you don't have time to do something, it simply isn't a high enough priority for you. That may seem harsh, but it is true.

I remember reading somewhere that in the 1950s a person's status was indicated by the amount of leisure time they had. The more free time, the higher their perceived status. These days, it seems like it is the other way around. People tell themselves and others how busy they are. It is like a badge of honour. Telling themselves and others how important and needed they are. Is that really the case? When people tell me how busy they are, I don't feel impressed, I genuinely feel quite sad because I know that more often than not, they are creating this 'busyness' for themselves.

Some people tell me that every minute of their working day is taken up with meetings, meaning that they only get to do their actual 'work' at night or on weekends. Really? Is every minute of every work day taken up with meetings that you must attend and therefore taking you away from being able to get things done? If so, then maybe you should reassess your employment, or have a good talk with your manager. And how critical is it that you actually do attend every single one of these meetings? If you answered 'critical', then ask yourself what would happen if you were sick one day? Or you had a major event in your life like getting married or a child of yours was getting married and you needed to travel for the event? Or how about an overseas trip that you had booked 12 months before? What would happen to those meetings then? Would the meetings be unable to go ahead? Would you never be able to get the information that you might have 'needed' from the meetings that you missed? Would the business/organisation be unable to cope without you? I suspect that is unlikely. Somehow, they would go on (yes, you do note a little sarcasm there).

Look, I have been there myself, so I know exactly what it feels like and how convinced you can be that you are 'so busy'. Fortunately for me, at the height of this busyness, when I felt so overwhelmed and could not see any way out of it, I read two excellent books (yes, somehow in the middle of all that 'being busy' I managed to find the time to read a book or two). One of those books in particular was literally life-changing in terms of managing my time. That particular book is *Eat that Frog!* by Brian Tracy. I read that book, and literally the next day started putting many of the strategies into place and immediately found that I had more time. Immediately.

To quote the back cover of my copy of *Eat that Frog!*: 'There *just isn't enough time for everything on our "To Do" list – and there never will be. Successful people don't try to do everything. They learn to focus on the most important tasks and make sure they get done.'*

The key message I took from *Eat that Frog!* is based on something Mark Twain said, that went along the lines of *'If the first thing you do each day is eat a live frog, then you can go through the rest of your day knowing that you have dealt with the worst thing you are going to have to do that day'*.

So, good news and bad news here. The bad news, that frog is the biggest, ugliest, worst job that you have on your 'To Do' list. It is the one that you really do not want to do. It is the one that plays on your mind all day (and each night). It is the phone call you don't want to make, the least favourite of your work tasks (for me it was always my monthly budget update) or the person that you have to have a conversation with (and you really don't want to).

The good news. Deal with this frog first and you will be amazed by how much time you get back. Time that is not spent using up energy thinking about the frogs that you have to deal with.

I read *Eat that Frog!* one weekend, and by Monday morning I had turned my 'To Do' list on its head. Instead of being so busy doing all the little things that I didn't have time for the big things, I now did all the big things first and found I had plenty of time for the little things. By the way, the other book I read shortly after this was *Busy* by Tony Crabbe. I would highly recommend it.

At this stage, just question your mindset around how busy you are. Are you really open to hearing and accepting that you can take control of your time, your career and your life?

I had a conversation recently with another consultant who is always 'busy'. He asked me how things were going and I was telling him how happy I am with the balance I have in my life, in particular being able to spend more time with my daughter while maintaining my business. He asked (a little incredulously) how I was doing it. I explained a few things that I was doing (naturally topics I have discussed in this book) and his response (sadly like many others I have heard) was along the lines of, 'Oh that wouldn't work for me, my situation is quite different'. Really? Is your situation, your career, or are you, really so unique that you cannot take control of all this busyness? Again, I would like to suggest that you consider how much your mindset is contributing to how busy you are and how busy you need to be. Another aspect worth thinking about is what I referred to in the chapter for *Strategy 2 – Take a Break*. Perhaps if you are so busy, it could be worth considering how much of this busyness you are creating yourself through setting up certain expectations in other people?

And if nothing else, apart from how it may be impacting your ability to achieve your goals, think about the effect this 'busyness' is having on those that you care about? Your children, your partner, your family? And if you don't think it is having any sort of negative impact, then I will ask you to think again.

How Finding the Time will allow you to achieve Success with Less Stress

Less stress

And isn't this sort of the point? Taking back control of your time will promptly lower your stress levels. You will experience fewer unexpected surprises, not as many tight deadlines, less rushing around from task to task or from meeting to meeting. You will also experience fewer problems such as a forgotten appointment or a missed deadline, all of which add to our stress levels and feelings of worry and anxiety.

More free time

Isn't that what we all want? We are all given the same amount of time in any given day, week or year, but no matter what your circumstances you can make better use of it. For example, when writing this book, I have done so first thing each morning. It saves my head from being full of all that I want to write throughout the day, and frees up my evenings and weekends for time with my daughter. Maybe for you that free time can be used for preparing to climb that mountain or to study for the qualification you have always wanted.

Improves your reputation and influence

I often work with new managers, teaching them the various skills of managing people. Many of these new managers find themselves inundated with a bunch of new responsibilities, additional meetings (always more meetings!) and then there is the actual job of managing and developing the people who work in their team. They are busy rushing from activity to activity and the stress and overwhelm can be seen all over their face and in their body language. If this sounds like you, think about the message you are sending to your team and to your own manager. Not a great one I suspect. By taking back control of your time, not only are you better placed to manage your day-to-day responsibilities and your people, but your reputation for being calm, in control and 'on top of things' will proceed you. This in turn will enable more opportunities for your own success goals, as you will be known as reliable, competent and capable.

Strategies for Finding the Time

DO

- *Avoid Mindless Acceptance Syndrome* (watch TED Talk below), and be more strategic about meetings you attend.

- *Re-write your 'To Do' list* in an order that will get you closer to your success goals. Put your biggest frog first.

- *At the end of each 'work' day, write your 'To Do' list for the next day* in the order suggested in the dot point above. Taking five minutes at the end of each day to write this will dramatically change how you manage your time. Yes, other things will invariably 'come up' but with a clearer focus on your priorities, you will be better placed and much more comfortable about whether or when you action those unexpected activities.

READ

- *Eat that Frog!* by Brian Tracy. Published by Berrett-Koehler 2017. Oakland CA

- *Busy — How to thrive in a world of too much* by Tony Crabbe. Published by Piatkus 2014. Great Britain

WATCH

- TED Talk — *How to save the world (or at least yourself) from bad meetings* by David Grady

Select a strategy from either Do, Read or Watch, or create one of your own and record it on the next page.

A strategy I will implement…

How will this enable me to achieve Success with Less Stress…

Strategy 7 — Not Procrastinating

On the morning that I started to write this chapter, I said to my sister that I should write a chapter on procrastination but that it would be hard for me to do so as I don't procrastinate so find it hard to understand the mindset. She said that maybe she should write the chapter as she is an expert at procrastination. I laughed and told her that was probably a great idea, the only problem being, that she is such a great procrastinator that the chapter would never get written!

I have always described myself as the opposite of a procrastinator, it turns out there has now been a term phrased for people like me which is *precrastination*. People have often told me that this is a good thing, because I have always been focused on getting things done and never left things unfinished. However, it did mean that I would rush at things like a bull at a gate and therefore not allow myself the time to let creativity come naturally.

Before I continue with this chapter, I would like to clarify: the type of procrastination I am referring to here is not the procrastination of 'starting quickly and continuing slowly' as described by Adam Grant in his TED Talk *The surprising habits of original thinkers*. There is great value in this concept of starting work on something and then taking a break (procrastinating a little) before continuing. I have learned the value of slowing down and have found my best ideas come to me when I am given a problem or a concept to work on and then let it sit in the back of my mind for a day or two. The type of procrastinating I am referring to here is when you know you have something that you need to do or should do and continue to delay getting started, like Tim Urban describes in his TED Talk, *Inside the mind of a master procrastinator*.

So, why do people procrastinate? There can be many reasons. Sometimes it is because people want things to be 'just right'; the right time, the right environment, the right person. Well, guess what? If you keep waiting for the right time, the right situation or the right person, it or they will never arrive. Never. Ever. You will always find some reason to put off what needs to be done. The stars are not going to align perfectly, signalling that now is the right time to do whatever it is you need to do. And think of all the potentially great opportunities and adventures you may be missing out on!

Let me give you an example. I have a friend who was recently engaged by a small business owner to market their products and services. This was an existing business that had done well for a while, and now they were struggling, mostly due to a lack of marketing and promotion. There was one particular product that this business owner wanted my friend to market, as it had the potential to provide a great return on her investment. My friend dutifully began her marketing campaign and literally within days, enquires and sales for this particular product completely skyrocketed. The business owner then called my friend in a panic. She wasn't sure that she wanted her to market this product anymore. My friend was perplexed? 'But this is what you asked me to market. This is what you have engaged me to do.' It turned out the reason the business owner was concerned was because she didn't think her product was 'perfect' yet.

Oh my! It is incredibly unlikely that any product or service you ever produce is going to be perfect! Look, deep down you really do know that nothing will be perfect, don't you? Sure, aim for excellent or fantastic or awesome, but the only way you are even going to achieve that is by getting out there and selling your products and services, starting to climb that mountain or writing that book/memo/report. It won't be perfect. In fact, the only way you can get to excellent or awesome is to get started, do what needs doing and learn from the mistakes, feedback and suggestions you get along the way. This book isn't perfect (the proof is in your hands). I don't expect it to be perfect, but if I felt I couldn't write and then publish it until it was perfect; well, you already know the answer. It would never be finished and it would never have been published.

How Not Procrastinating can help you achieve Success with Less Stress

You will accomplish *something*

It might not be the end result you were aiming for. However, doing something, anything, that moves you towards your success goals will mean that you achieve something. Let's say it's that mountain you want to climb. Well, getting outside and going for a walk will do a bunch of things for you. It will inspire you to get outside and walk again (maybe at least part way up that mountain). It will help you to work out whether your walking shoes are appropriate or it will let you know how much further effort you need to put into your current fitness levels. Let's say you have always wanted to visit Japan. Well apart from the obvious, booking your trip, you could find a cheap or free app or book and start learning to speak Japanese. All the while saving for your trip of a lifetime.

You can achieve other things

Everything and anything that you do, will help you to achieve other things. I used to talk about this with job seekers (when I worked in recruitment) who were looking for or waiting for, the perfect job to apply for. By the way, the perfect job is incredibly rare and most people don't just walk into them when they become available. As I would say to my job seekers, every job you do teaches you something that you can then take to the next job or allows you to apply and have a better chance at that 'perfect' job. When you don't procrastinate, and you get things done, your time and your mind's energy are then free to move on to achieve other (and often more exciting) things.

You will have more time to work on your success goals

This is particularly the case when procrastination leads us down that slippery slope of short-term gratification, such as checking Facebook, instead of writing that report. Eventually that report will need to be written and the time we wasted on doing things that we really didn't have to do will need to be paid back with that report writing. If you can focus on starting the task at hand (and not procrastinating), you will finish it quicker and give yourself the time and freedom to do the things that you would really rather be doing.

Strategies for Not Procrastinating

DO

- *Something!* Anything that takes you one step further to your success goals. Stop thinking about it and actually do it. Right now. In fact, don't even read this book any further until you have done something tangible that takes you closer to your goals.

- *Engage (paid or unpaid) an Accountability Buddy.* Find someone who will help you to stay on track and be accountable for what you need to do and get done. It could be a colleague, a coach, a friend or your personal partner (though there is a risk if you engage your personal partner that you may start to view their reminders and follow-ups as *nagging*).

READ

- *Feel the Fear and Do it Anyway* by Susan J. Jeffers. Published by Ebury Publishing 2012. United Kingdom

WATCH

- TED Talk — *Inside the mind of a master procrastinator* by Tim Urban

- TED Talk — *The surprising habits of original thinkers* by Adam Grant

Select a strategy from either Do, Read or Watch, or create one of your own and record it on the next page.

A strategy I will implement…

How will this enable me to achieve Success with Less Stress…

Strategy 8 — The Voice in Your Head

I want to talk with you about that voice in your head. You know the one, it's always there. The one that reminds you that you 'cannot' do something or that you have never been any good at something else... 'I can't sing, I am useless at maths, I have a terrible sense of direction', and so it goes...

Our brain is quite incredible. We tell ourselves stories all the time and our brain accepts these stories as true or fact, until or unless, we tell it otherwise. Mostly we do not even recognise that we are telling ourselves these stories. The thing is, these stories can be holding us back from achieving success or being able to do the things we really would like to be doing.

To this end, we end up creating our own versions of 'reality'. But, what is reality, really? In any given moment, reality can be changed because reality is based on the observer or individual. We know that through the varying accounts that eyewitnesses give at any given crime scene. Five different witnesses can mean five different accounts of what did or did not happen. Our reality is merely our brain's understanding of the world, which is based on our own and individual experiences, beliefs and self-talk.

Think about this: it is said that on average we verbalise about 16,000 words a day and we have anywhere from 50,000 to 70,000 thoughts per day. Now think about all those thoughts. How many of those do you think are factual, and how many of them are assumptions, judgements or stories we are telling ourselves. Just think about that for a moment.

To add to our assumptions, judgements and stories, all of these thoughts are interlaced with complex emotions. Some are positive and helpful, such as: 'I've worked hard on this report and will ace the presentation at today's Board Meeting'. Others are negative and less helpful, such as: 'She doesn't like me, I am useless at data analysis, Why am I always the one who (insert your own, why does this always happen to me here)?'

It is important to recognise that we can change that perspective at any moment. I have a ton of favourite TED Talks (you may very well have gathered this already by reading through my 'Watch' suggestions). One of my all-time favourites is *The Happy Secret to Better Work*, by Shawn Anchor. In that talk, he says: *'We're finding it's not necessarily the reality that shapes us, but the lens through which your brain views the world that shapes your reality. And if we can change the lens, not only can we change your happiness, we can change every single educational and business outcome at the same time.'*

Let me give you an example, one that most people will relate to, as many people have a strong aversion to the idea of speaking in public.

I had a colleague approach me once and ask me 'who was the worst-case scenario I had ever worked with, in terms of a person not being able to speak in public, and who then went on to become a public speaker.' I laughed and said 'well, that would have been me'. I then went on to explain my story to her. Up until my mid-twenties, the mere thought of speaking to a group of people terrified me. If I had to speak to a group, I would physically sweat and shake and my voice would stammer so much, I could barely get words out. It was awful. I can still see the looks on people's faces, which tended to be more horror than pity. I couldn't even sit with a group of people at a table and contribute to a conversation. Fortunately for me, I recognised that this wasn't helping me at all and I engaged a coach and attended public speaking groups and learned how to speak in public. It certainly wasn't easy and the only way to learn how to do this is to actually speak in public. However, I then went on (a very short time after that) to start a career that required me to speak in front of groups of people every single day and I loved it and continue to love it. In fact, I couldn't have had the career I have had and all the wonderful experiences I have enjoyed without having learned to speak in public.

Having said that, my story is not the example I want to highlight in this chapter. Rather it is my colleague's story when she approached me and what followed. After I gave her a brief overview of my own story, she said to me. 'I know that in order to progress in my career I need to learn how to speak in public.' She then went on to say in a very strong and certain voice, 'However, I will never be able to speak in public'. I stopped her right there. Can you see what she was doing? Did you hear what she said? Every time she thought to herself or said out loud 'I will never be able to speak in public' her mind replied 'ok'. She was giving herself permission to not even try, because she 'knew' she would never be able to do it. I asked her to simply change what she was telling herself. Instead of saying 'I will never be able to speak in public' I suggested she say, 'I am not comfortable speaking in public yet'. That simple rewording, and in particular, adding 'yet', can be very powerful. It tells your mind that this thing (you used to say you could never do) is now a possibility and likely to be doable in the future.

I was so proud of my colleague. Not only did she take my suggestion on board, but three weeks later she came to see me and told me that she had enrolled in Toastmasters (an organisation that teaches public speaking skills). Naturally, she was still very nervous about public speaking and told me that she planned to attend a few meetings and give herself permission to get up and speak when she felt ready. Notice the 'when' rather than 'if'? It was less than a month later that she came to see me and excitedly told me that she had spoken to the group at her Toastmasters meeting the night before. I could not have been happier for her. In less than two months, she had gone from someone who 'would never' be able to speak in public, to someone who had spoken in public and would go on to learn to become very comfortable with it and end up enjoying it.

So, what are the stories you are telling yourself? Are you: not creative, can't dance, can't sing, terrible at maths, no good at sport? Maybe, in order to achieve your success goals, it is time to change the story you are telling yourself by changing your language.

How changing that Voice in Your Head can help you achieve Success with Less Stress

You will achieve the things you thought were not possible

Just like my colleague who used to say, 'I will never be able to speak in public' and now can, you too can learn to do or achieve whatever it is that you want to do. Assuming you want to that is. For example, I will often say that I am terrible at maths. I don't even try to change my self-talk in that area because I simply have no interest in learning to become better at maths. However, at the same time, I recognise every time I say that I am terrible at maths, it is because I choose to be. It is not some innate fault within me. You can learn and do whatever is needed to achieve your success goals. I could learn to be good at maths if I wanted to. Remember the research referred to by Shawn Anchor: a positive lens improves performance and productivity. Your intelligence rises, creativity rises and your energy levels rise.

You will change those self-limiting beliefs

A quote I often use when people say to me 'I can't' is one by Henry Ford, who said something similar to the following: *'Whether you think you can, or whether you think you can't, either way, you are right.'*

When I first started to think about writing this book, I delayed for quite some time. I kept saying to myself 'Who am I to write this book?' My reasoning was that there are lots of people out there, who are no doubt more qualified than me who could write on this topic. While that is most likely true, they are not (as far as I am aware) writing this book. I then started thinking about and focusing on the feedback I receive from the participants in my programs when I facilitate training on these very topics. I began to remind myself about the appreciation from my learners and how positively they respond to what they learn from me. I then started saying to myself 'People love learning this from me. How is writing a book on these topics any different from writing a training program?' And from there, I commenced writing this book.

Live longer and be healthier

True, based on research from The Mayo Clinic. The Mayo Clinic is a not-for profit organisation, focused on clinic practice, education and research, and, according to their website, was one of the top-ranking hospitals in the US for 2016–17. According to them, the health benefits of positive thinking, which starts with positive self-talk, include:

- Increased life span
- Lower rates of depression
- Lower levels of distress
- Greater resistance to the common cold
- Better psychological and physical wellbeing
- Better cardiovascular health and reduced risk of death from cardiovascular disease
- Better coping skills during hardships and times of stress

Now, that sounds pretty good to me.

Source: www.mayoclinic.org/healthy-lifestyle/stress-management/in-depth/positive-thinking/art-20043950

Strategies for the Voice in your Head

DO

- *Start noticing the stories you are telling yourself.* Catch yourself next time you say either to yourself or out loud 'I can't' or 'I am terrible at...' And practice positively reframing your thoughts and words. It might help you to write down those negative self-talk statements and then rewrite them as positive self-talk. This means when you catch yourself in the act, you know how you want to reframe that thought.

- *Develop some insight into yourself* through the free questionnaires that are available via the Authentic Happiness website. www.authentichappiness.sas.upenn.edu/testcenter

READ

- *Mindset, The New Psychology of Success* by Carol Dweck. Published by Little, Brown Book Group 2017. United Kingdom

- *Learned Optimism – How to Change Your Mind and Your Life* by Martin E. P. Seligman. Published by Vintage Books 2006. US

- *Self-Talk your way to Success.* By Kamran Akhter

WATCH

- TEDx Talk – *Change your story, change your life* by Sarah Vaid

- TEDx Talk — *The imposter syndrome* by Kirsty Walker

Select a strategy from either Do, Read or Watch, or create one of your own and record it on the next page.

> A strategy I will implement…

> How will this enable me to achieve Success with Less Stress…

Strategy 9 — Engage a Coach or Mentor

There are very few people (in fact none that I can think of) that succeed completely on their own. Think of anyone you consider successful, be it someone you know personally, or someone 'famous', like a sports star or celebrity. They have all had support from other people in one way or another to achieve what they want to achieve. I am sure you have read or watched many an interview where the subject in question was being asked about their success or achievements and they have said something along the lines of 'I couldn't have done it without...'

No matter how capable you may feel, you simply do not have all the answers. There is always someone who can better guide you, challenge you or simply point you in the right direction. Regardless of what your success goal is, unless perhaps your goal is to be the first human being on Mars, then someone else has already done it and achieved it. Save yourself time and frustration by learning from their mistakes and find someone who has done it before and is happy to share their valuable advice and guidance. In fact, even if your success goal *is* to be the first human being on Mars, there will still be someone who has spent extended time in space or who has explored harsh environments with limited resources. The point is, whatever it is you want to do, you don't need to do it on your own.

With this in mind, I suggest that you engage either a coach or a mentor or both. You might be asking, is there a difference between a coach and a mentor. Well, yes there is. A coach is usually someone who can help you develop a specific skill set for a task, activity or challenge that you want to overcome. Think of a sports coach who coaches their team or individuals to perform at a certain skill level. They are working to direct their team to a specific standard or result (such as winning a grand final). A mentor tends to be someone who has either a personal interest in you, or a personal interest in helping others. A mentor tends to have experience in the area you wish to grow in and rather than directing you to focus on a particular skill set, they will provide information, knowledge or advice and most importantly, challenge and question you.

Does it cost money to engage a coach or a mentor? The answer is sometimes yes and sometimes no. You may be fortunate enough to work in an organisation that employs people who either take on a coaching role as part of their job description or others (usually more senior people) who are happy to take on the role of mentor. Then again, it depends on what you are aiming to achieve. If it is to climb that mountain, then you will most likely need to look outside of your organisation or work environment to find someone who can help you.

I am incredibly fortunate. As this chapter started to form, I was flooded with images and memories of past and present coaches and mentors. Some as far back as 25 years ago when I was working with Ansett Australia. Percy, if you are out there, I have always wanted to say thank you for the mentoring and challenges you gave me. I have never forgotten. And others more recent, such as the lovely Ian Whitehouse who I have known for about 10 years now and who has always freely (and patiently!) given up his time to coach me in technical and business-related skills.

As recently as within the past month, I sought out and then participated in both a coaching session and a mentoring conversation. Both of which provided me with tangible information, skills and knowledge to help me achieve some current goals. The coach I paid for. My husband nearly had a meltdown when I told him the cost of engaging the coach, however, as to be expected, the financial investment was worthwhile. I am always aware that I 'don't know what I don't know'. The coach I engaged focuses on business coaching and I wanted to be sure that I was doing all that I need, to ensure my business remains sustainable.

My coach focused on some specific skill sets that I was unsure of, and thankfully, provided me with honest and challenging feedback around some of my activities (thank you Heidi Modorovich!). Trust me, honest feedback is worth its weight in gold. Some people become uncomfortable at the thought of getting feedback that shines a light on their shortcomings, however there is huge value in this. Think about it: how many times in your life have you looked back at a particular situation or challenging time and thought 'if only I had known...' or 'if only someone had told me...' Please, welcome feedback with an open and curious mind. It is a wonderful opportunity.

Then in the same week I was writing this chapter, I had a fantastic mentoring conversation with a colleague (thank you Kylie Dunn!) who is an experienced writer, editor and has traversed the tricky world of self-publishing. In this instance, I asked for her advice as I knew that there was a lot that I didn't know about how to publish a book, but boy did I find out that there was just so much I didn't know! She was kind enough to give up some of her time and share with me her experience, suggestions and resources, as well as asking me a bunch of questions that really got me thinking. Without going into all the detail, before our conversation, I thought I had it all sorted. I had 'worked it out' for myself and I thought she might have a few tips for me. To cut a long dialogue short, that mentoring conversation has saved me from a world of stress when it comes to publishing this book. I now have the information, knowledge and resources I need to make the process as straightforward and stress-free as possible for myself. So, in terms of a current goal (publishing this book), I will now be able to do so with a lot less stress.

No matter what you want to achieve, be it developing technical skills or knowledge, running your own financially sustainable business, moving up the corporate ladder or enhancing your communication skills or self-confidence, a coach or a mentor can help you with this.

You might be thinking to yourself — 'But how do I find a

coach or mentor?' Well, they are everywhere. Firstly, get clear about your success goal and the skills, knowledge or capability that you need to develop in order to achieve it. Then ascertain whether you need a coach (more likely if it is a specific skill you need), or a mentor (more likely if you need knowledge or wise counsel). You then might like to start by considering your own network and people you already know who have the skills, attributes, knowledge or experience who can help you. If you are looking for an informal coaching/mentoring relationship within your own network (remember your network extends across family, friends, friends of friends, work colleagues, sporting clubs and educational institutes such as university if you are studying), most people that you ask are going to be flattered and respond well to your request. If your own network is not an option then consider joining a professional membership organisation that has coaching or mentoring service offerings. If you are looking for a mentor, (and you are in Australia) the Australian Government Website has a page dedicated to mentoring services for business (www.business.gov.au). If you are looking for a coach, the International Coaching Federation has an extensive member directory with global reach.

How Engaging a Coach will help you achieve Success with Less Stress

Enhanced skill and ability

According to the International Coaching Federation, '80% of people who receive coaching report increased self-confidence, and over 70% benefit from improved work performance, relationships, and more effective communication skills.'

Increased accountability

Having a coach will hold you accountable to your plan for achieving your success goals. A good coach will ask you for updates on your progress. A good coach will also ask you a lot of questions (rather than telling you what to do), so that you can take responsibility for either achieving your goals or being honest about what was not achieved.

How Engaging a Mentor will help you achieve Success with Less Stress

A fresh perspective

A great mentor will challenge you and stretch your thinking. They can provide you with a fresh perspective, different from your own, as they have usually 'been through it all before'. (Think of my mentor who is a writer, editor and publisher). With their experience, they can give you insight about the lessons they have learned along the way.

Industry or environment knowledge and contacts

This can be a fantastic benefit of engaging a mentor. A good mentor will have experience in the industry or environment you wish to grow in and more often than not, be able (and willing) to offer personal introductions to their contacts. Your mentor may have spent years building these relationships, which may not otherwise have been available to you.

Strategies for Engaging a Coach or Mentor

DO

- *Ascertain the specific skills or knowledge you need* to help you achieve your success goals, then engage a coach or mentor.
- If you don't wish to engage a coach or mentor, *at least seek advice or guidance* from others who have already achieved what you are aiming for.

READ

- *Coaching for Resilience, A Practical Guide to Using Positive Psychology* by Adrienne Green and John Humphrey. Published by Kogan Page Ltd 2012. Great Britain and US
- International Coaching Federation — *Need a Coach?* www.coachfederation.org

WATCH

- TED Talk — *How to get better at the things you care about* by Eduardo Biceno

Select a strategy from either Do, Read or Watch, or create one of your own and record it on the next page.

- A strategy I will implement...

How will this enable me to achieve Success with Less Stress...

The Difference This All Makes

'You are not going to master the rest of your life in one day. Just relax. Master the day. Then just keep doing that every day.'
www.peacefulmindpeacefullife.org

A friend asked me why I wasn't curled up in a corner in the foetal position? It had been a tough week. Apart from the usual ups and downs of life, work and family, a couple of major events had occurred.

My sister suffers from diagnosed depression and anxiety. At this particular time, she had experienced some extremely traumatic events in her life. My mother called me late one evening, very concerned about my sister's mental state and asked me to go check on her. When I arrived at my sister's home, she was hysterical and wanted to end her life. I managed to convince her that she needed professional help and took her to the emergency section of the local hospital. I waited with her while a mental health nurse spoke with her and then sat with her through most of the night until the hospital was able to confirm they would find a bed for her. Due to a lack of hospital beds, she was kept in a bed in the emergency area for two days before they could move her to one of the psychiatric wards. We agreed that when she was feeling better and released from hospital, that she and her daughter would come and live with myself, my husband and daughter for a while. That period of living with us would be several months. After a few days, my sister was released from hospital with new medication and moved in with us. I am happy to say that she is doing well, and she was also happy for me to talk about this event in this book. We both know the value in more people openly talking about mental health difficulties and the potentially devastating effects it can have.

Two days after my sister was released from hospital, we experienced another traumatic event.

My husband and I had gone into a partnership and had bought a pub (bar and bistro) nine months earlier. Owning a pub is a lot of work. The pub is a seven-day-a-week business and my husband was averaging 90 hours a week, which was to be expected when getting a new business like that running smoothly. This business was also about to become our only source of regular income, as that was the week I was finishing my full-time employment as an employee and stepping into the world of becoming fully self-employed as a consultant.

For some reason, I woke at about 2:00am. I got up and found my husband sitting at the computer in our home office. He looked at me and said, 'Fire'. In my half-asleep state, I misunderstood him and thought he said 'Five' as in five thousand, and that he was referring to an invoice that needed to be paid. 'Five thousand?' I asked? 'No' he said looking at me with a terrible look. 'Fire'.

Due to an electrical fault, our pub had caught on fire that night. Thankfully it was after closing time and no-one was hurt, however the fire was serious and had caused hundreds of thousands of dollars in damage. It was to turn out that we wouldn't be able to open and trade for many months. Naturally, I felt shock as he relayed to me the events of that evening. I remember thoughts running through my head like, are we going to lose our house? However, as early as the next day, I found myself reassuring my husband that everything would be ok and something positive would come out of this.

We were very grateful for the support and genuine concern that we received from friends and family in the days following the fire. At the same time, I simply wasn't experiencing the levels of stress that most people were expecting I would be feeling after a week of such distressing events. Hence my friend's question, 'Why aren't you curled up in the corner in the foetal position?'

My response to her was that I genuinely practise what I preach and that I was looking after myself. In particular, at such times, I am very focused on self-awareness. What am I feeling? Why am I feeling it? Is this helping or hindering me? And then consciously choosing a healthy state of being. Between that awareness and the strategies that I implement daily such as good sleep, taking mental breaks and minimalising the distractions in my life, I was well-placed to support my husband through the months (and the ups and downs that come with rebuilding a business both physically and financially) and to ensure that my daughter's day-to-day life was not impacted. She knew there was a fire and that the pub was closed for some time, however, she did not have to experience any flow-on stress or worry by having parents who were stressed out and unable to focus on her and her needs and wants.

I have written this book because as I said at the start, I come across so many people that are stressed out, on the edge of burning out and feeling like they are just chasing their tails and not getting anywhere. Honestly, it doesn't have to be that way. Yes, life is going to throw us some curve balls and things will happen that may divert us away from our goals for a while. I think it is important to remember that we usually have more choices than we often tell ourselves.

Nothing would make me happier than hearing from you, the reader, that something you implemented after reading this book, has helped you to achieve your goals or taken you even just one step closer to your version of success. Feel free to contact me via my website successwithlessstress.com.au or email contact@successwithlessstress.com.au

From the bottom of my heart, I genuinely wish you the best and that you can find **'Success with Less Stress'**.

Remember to visit

successwithlessstress.com.au/resources/

to access all the talks listed in the book.

About the Author

Rachel is an adventurer, traveller and lifelong learner. In her professional life, she is a highly skilled facilitator and coach with a passion for helping people to be successful and happy in their careers.

Success with Less Stress was founded out of a genuine desire to help individuals and teams develop their self-management and relationship management skills and to enhance their professional performance and career success.

Rachel is passionate about helping people to develop their levels of self-awareness as well as acquiring healthy self-management strategies. In her professional work, she chooses to focus on educating in the areas of health and wellbeing, emotional intelligence, stress management and resilience. In her personal life, she practices what she teaches.

Find out more about Rachel and her work at www.successwithlessstress.com.au.

www.ingramcontent.com/pod-product-compliance
Lightning Source LLC
Chambersburg PA
CBHW072101290426
44110CB00014B/1781